SCOTTISH SONGS

15 HIGHLAND TUNES ARRANGED BY PHILLIP KEVEREN

```
— PIANO LEVEL —
INTERMEDIATE
```

ISBN 978-1-5400-4668-0

Visit Hal Leonard Online at
www.halleonard.com

Visit Phillip at
www.phillipkeveren.com

Contact us:
Hal Leonard
7777 West Bluemound Road
Milwaukee, WI 53213
Email: info@halleonard.com

In Europe, contact:
Hal Leonard Europe Limited
42 Wigmore Street
Marylebone, London, W1U 2RN
Email: info@halleonardeurope.com

In Australia, contact:
Hal Leonard Australia Pty. Ltd.
4 Lentara Court
Cheltenham, Victoria, 3192 Australia
Email: info@halleonard.com.au

PREFACE

I have always been drawn to folk songs. There is something about their authentic, transparent nature that is refreshing and inspiring. The songs in this collection were chosen for both inherent beauty and suitability to piano solo adaptation.

As you prepare to learn these arrangements, I would recommend seeking out and listening to a performance (vocal, if possible) of the tune. This will enlighten your interpretation at the piano.

Sincerely,

Phillip Keveren

BIOGRAPHY

Phillip Keveren, a multi-talented keyboard artist and composer, has composed original works in a variety of genres from piano solo to symphonic orchestra. He gives frequent concerts and workshops for teachers and their students in the United States, Canada, Europe, and Asia. Mr. Keveren holds a B.M. in composition from California State University Northridge and a M.M. in composition from the University of Southern California.

CONTENTS

AULD LANG SYNE

Words by ROBERT BURNS
Traditional Scottish Melody
Arranged by Phillip Keveren

BARBARA ALLEN

Traditional English
Arranged by Phillip Keveren

THE BLUE BELLS OF SCOTLAND

Words and Music attributed to MRS. JORDON
Arranged by Phillip Keveren

THE CAMPBELLS ARE COMING

Scottish Folksong
Arranged by Phillip Keveren

LOCH LOMOND

Scottish Folksong
Arranged by Phillip Keveren

14

CHARLIE IS MY DARLIN'

Lyrics by JAMES HOGG
and LADY CAROLINA NAIRNE
Folk Melody
Arranged by Phillip Keveren

COMIN' THROUGH THE RYE

Traditional Scottish Melody
Arranged by Phillip Keveren

19

A HIGHLAND LAD MY LOVE WAS BORN

Traditional Folk Melody
Lyrics by ROBERT BURNS
Arranged by Phillip Keveren

HURREE HURROO

Scottish Folksong
Arranged by Phillip Keveren

MINGULAY BOAT SONG

Words and Music by SIR HUGH S. ROBERTON
Arranged by Phillip Keveren

O MY LOVE IS LIKE A RED, RED ROSE

Traditional Folk Melody
Lyrics by ROBERT BURNS
Arranged by Phillip Keveren

YE BANKS AND BRAES O' BONNIE DOON

Lyrics by ROBERT BURNS
Melody by CHARLES MILLER
Arranged by Phillip Keveren

Driving (♩. = 63)

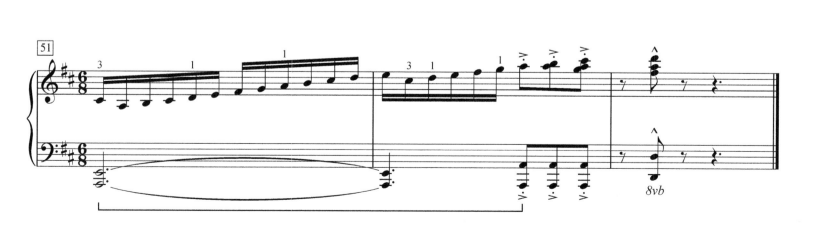

ON THE BANKS OF ALLAN WATER

By MATTHEW GREGORY LEWIS
Arranged by Phillip Keveren

With melancholy (♩ = c. 76-80)

THE ROAD TO DUNDEE

Traditional Scottish Folk Ballad
Arranged by Phillip Keveren

SKYE BOAT SONG

Words by ROBERT LOUIS STEVENSON
Traditional Scottish Melody
Arranged by Phillip Keveren

COMPOSER SHOWCASE
HAL LEONARD STUDENT PIANO LIBRARY

This series showcases great original piano music from our **Hal Leonard Student Piano Library** family of composers. Carefully graded for easy selection.

BILL BOYD

JAZZ BITS (AND PIECES)
Early Intermediate Level
00290312 11 Solos......................$7.99

JAZZ DELIGHTS
Intermediate Level
00240435 11 Solos......................$8.99

JAZZ FEST
Intermediate Level
00240436 10 Solos......................$8.99

JAZZ PRELIMS
Early Elementary Level
00290032 12 Solos......................$7.99

JAZZ SKETCHES
Intermediate Level
00220001 8 Solos.........................$8.99

JAZZ STARTERS
Elementary Level
00290425 10 Solos......................$8.99

JAZZ STARTERS II
Late Elementary Level
00290434 11 Solos......................$7.99

JAZZ STARTERS III
Late Elementary Level
00290465 12 Solos......................$8.99

THINK JAZZ!
Early Intermediate Level
00290417 Method Book............$12.99

TONY CARAMIA

JAZZ MOODS
Intermediate Level
00296728 8 Solos.........................$6.95

SUITE DREAMS
Intermediate Level
00296775 4 Solos.........................$6.99

SONDRA CLARK

DAKOTA DAYS
Intermediate Level
00296521 5 Solos.........................$6.95

FLORIDA FANTASY SUITE
Intermediate Level
00296766 3 Duets........................$7.95

THREE ODD METERS
Intermediate Level
00296472 3 Duets........................$6.95

MATTHEW EDWARDS

**CONCERTO FOR
YOUNG PIANISTS**
FOR 2 PIANOS, FOUR HANDS
Intermediate Level Book/CD
00296356 3 Movements $19.99

CONCERTO NO. 2 IN G MAJOR
FOR 2 PIANOS, 4 HANDS
Intermediate Level Book/CD
00296670 3 Movements............$17.99

PHILLIP KEVEREN

MOUSE ON A MIRROR
Late Elementary Level
00296361 5 Solos.........................$8.99

MUSICAL MOODS
Elementary/Late Elementary Level
00296714 7 Solos.........................$6.99

SHIFTY-EYED BLUES
Late Elementary Level
00296374 5 Solos.........................$7.99

CAROL KLOSE

THE BEST OF CAROL KLOSE
Early to Late Intermediate Level
00146151 15 Solos....................$12.99

CORAL REEF SUITE
Late Elementary Level
00296354 7 Solos.........................$7.50

DESERT SUITE
Intermediate Level
00296667 6 Solos.........................$7.99

FANCIFUL WALTZES
Early Intermediate Level
00296473 5 Solos.........................$7.95

GARDEN TREASURES
Late Intermediate Level
00296787 5 Solos.........................$8.50

ROMANTIC EXPRESSIONS
Intermediate to Late Intermediate Level
00296923 5 Solos.........................$8.99

WATERCOLOR MINIATURES
Early Intermediate Level
00296848 7 Solos.........................$7.99

JENNIFER LINN

AMERICAN IMPRESSIONS
Intermediate Level
00296471 6 Solos.........................$8.99

ANIMALS HAVE FEELINGS TOO
Early Elementary/Elementary Level
00147789 8 Solos.........................$8.99

AU CHOCOLAT
Late Elementary/Early Intermediate Level
00298110 7 Solos.........................$8.99

CHRISTMAS IMPRESSIONS
Intermediate Level
00296706 8 Solos.........................$8.99

JUST PINK
Elementary Level
00296722 9 Solos.........................$8.99

LES PETITES IMAGES
Late Elementary Level
00296664 7 Solos.........................$8.99

LES PETITES IMPRESSIONS
Intermediate Level
00296355 6 Solos.........................$8.99

REFLECTIONS
Late Intermediate Level
00296843 5 Solos.........................$8.99

TALES OF MYSTERY
Intermediate Level
00296769 6 Solos.........................$8.99

LYNDA LYBECK-ROBINSON

ALASKA SKETCHES
Early Intermediate Level
00119637 8 Solos.........................$8.99

AN AWESOME ADVENTURE
Late Elementary Level
00137563 8 Solos.........................$7.99

FOR THE BIRDS
Early Intermediate/Intermediate Level
00237078 9 Solos.........................$8.99

WHISPERING WOODS
Late Elementary Level
00275905 9 Solos.........................$8.99

MONA REJINO

CIRCUS SUITE
Late Elementary Level
00296665 5 Solos.........................$8.99

COLOR WHEEL
Early Intermediate Level
00201951 6 Solos.........................$9.99

IMPRESIONES DE ESPAÑA
Intermediate Level
00337520 6 Solos.........................$8.99

IMPRESSIONS OF NEW YORK
Intermediate Level
00364212.....................................$8.99

JUST FOR KIDS
Elementary Level
00296840 8 Solos.........................$7.99

MERRY CHRISTMAS MEDLEYS
Intermediate Level
00296799 5 Solos.........................$8.99

MINIATURES IN STYLE
Intermediate Level
00148088 6 Solos.........................$8.99

PORTRAITS IN STYLE
Early Intermediate Level
00296507 6 Solos.........................$8.99

EUGÉNIE ROCHEROLLE

CELEBRATION SUITE
Intermediate Level
00152724 3 Duets........................$8.99

**ENCANTOS ESPAÑOLES
(SPANISH DELIGHTS)**
Intermediate Level
00125451 6 Solos.........................$8.99

JAMBALAYA
Intermediate Level
00296654 2 Pianos, 8 Hands.....$12.99
00296725 2 Pianos, 4 Hands.......$7.95

JEROME KERN CLASSICS
Intermediate Level
00296577 10 Solos....................$12.99

LITTLE BLUES CONCERTO
Early Intermediate Level
00142801 2 Pianos, 4 Hands......$12.99

TOUR FOR TWO
Late Elementary Level
00296832 6 Duets.......................$9.99

TREASURES
Late Elementary/Early Intermediate Level
00296924 7 Solos.........................$8.99

JEREMY SISKIND

BIG APPLE JAZZ
Intermediate Level
00278209 8 Solos.........................$8.99

MYTHS AND MONSTERS
Late Elementary/Early Intermediate Level
00148148 9 Solos.........................$8.99

CHRISTOS TSITSAROS

**DANCES FROM AROUND
THE WORLD**
Early Intermediate Level
00296688 7 Solos.........................$8.99

FIVE SUMMER PIECES
Late Intermediate/Advanced Level
00361235 5 Solos.......................$12.99

LYRIC BALLADS
Intermediate/Late Intermediate Level
00102404 6 Solos.........................$8.99

POETIC MOMENTS
Intermediate Level
00296403 8 Solos.........................$8.99

SEA DIARY
Early Intermediate Level
00253486 9 Solos.........................$8.99

SONATINA HUMORESQUE
Late Intermediate Level
00296772 3 Movements............$6.99

SONGS WITHOUT WORDS
Intermediate Level
00296506 9 Solos.........................$9.99

THREE PRELUDES
Early Advanced Level
00130747 3 Solos.........................$8.99

THROUGHOUT THE YEAR
Late Elementary Level
00296723 12 Duets.....................$6.95

ADDITIONAL COLLECTIONS

AT THE LAKE
by Elvina Pearce
Elementary/Late Elementary Level
00131642 10 Solos and Duets.....$7.99

CHRISTMAS FOR TWO
by Dan Fox
Early Intermediate Level
00290069 13 Duets....................$8.99

CHRISTMAS JAZZ
by Mike Springer
Intermediate Level
00296525 6 Solos.........................$8.99

COUNTY RAGTIME FESTIVAL
by Fred Kern
Intermediate Level
00296882 7 Solos.........................$7.99

LITTLE JAZZERS
by Jennifer Watts
Elementary/Late Elementary Level
00154573 9 Solos.........................$8.99

PLAY THE BLUES!
by Luann Carman
Early Intermediate Level
00296357 10 Solos.....................$9.99

ROLLER COASTERS & RIDES
by Jennifer & Mike Watts
Intermediate Level
00131144 8 Duets.......................$8.99

HAL•LEONARD®
www.halleonard.com

Prices, contents, and availability subject
to change without notice.

THE PHILLIP KEVEREN SERIES

PIANO SOLO

Prices, contents, and availability subject to change without notice.

0422
158